THE WORLD OF
Science

THE WORLD OF
Science

WORLD INTERNATIONAL PUBLISHING LIMITED
MANCHESTER

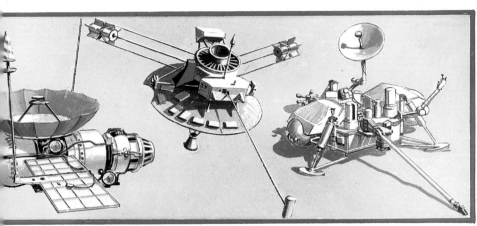

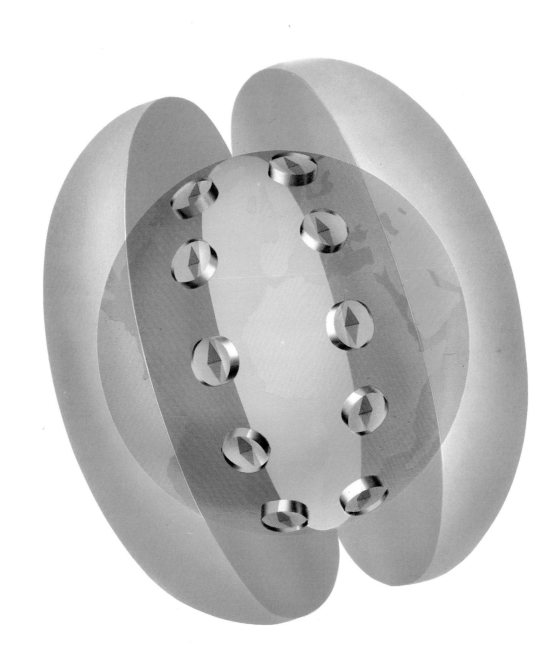

Contents

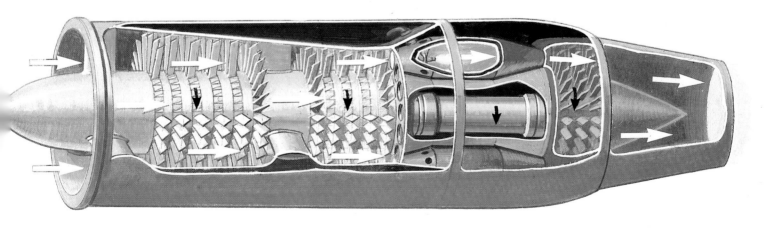

Solids, Liquids and Gases

When scientists talk about matter, they mean everything in the world. And all matter can be divided into three groups: solids such as iron or wood, liquids such as water and oil, and gases such as air or steam. Ice is solid water. When ice is heated it melts to become liquid water. When the liquid is heated to 100°C it boils and becomes a gas – steam.

Solids tend to resist being pulled or pushed out of shape; they usually keep the same size and shape, no matter where they are. Liquids have no shape of their own. They take the shape of any container they are poured into. Gases do not keep either their shape or their size. They expand to completely fill anything they are in.

The reason why different materials behave in different ways is because of the tiny atoms that make them up. Iron is different from gold because it is made up of a different kind of atom. The way in which the atoms are packed together decides whether a substance is a solid, a liquid or a gas.

Water is a strange liquid. It is one of the very few things that grows bigger (expands) when it freezes. That is why huge icebergs float, even though most of the bulk is under the surface.

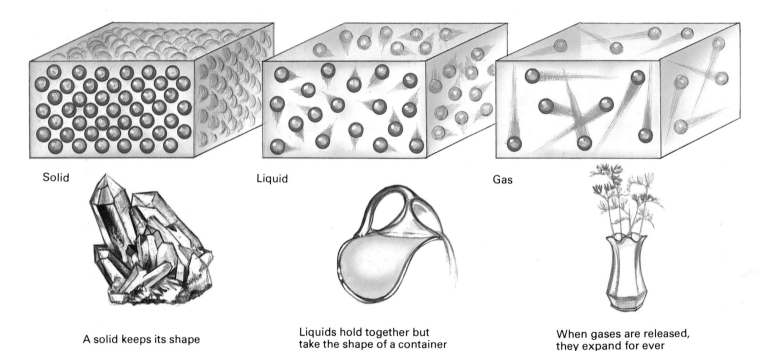

Solid

Liquid

Gas

A solid keeps its shape

Liquids hold together but take the shape of a container

When gases are released, they expand for ever

How solid something is depends on how closely packed the atoms in it are. In a solid, the atoms are close together and fixed in position. This is why it is difficult for a solid to change its shape or its size. In a liquid, the atoms are less tightly packed and can move about a bit.

When a solid is heated, the atoms in it move more and more until they form a liquid. They move apart but do not escape from each other completely. If we go on heating a liquid, the particles in it move faster and faster. After a while they move so quickly that they escape from the surface of the liquid and become a gas. This is called *evaporation*. When the liquid gets hotter still, the particles escape so quickly that the liquid bubbles. This is called *boiling*. When water boils it turns into the invisible gas, steam.

Solids

Solids are solid because of the way their atoms and molecules are arranged. Ice, water and steam are all the same from a chemical point of view – they all contain the same kind of atoms and molecules. The difference lies in the movement of the molecules. In ice, the molecules are held tightly in a definite pattern – what is called a *crystal lattice* – by strong forces between the neighbouring molecules. Snow is a mass of beautiful ice crystals, each six-sided and no two of them are alike (see above). Although molecules in ice do not move about, they still vibrate a little.

Liquids

Some substances such as water, oil and the metal mercury are liquid at ordinary room temperature. A liquid is similar to a gas because its atoms and molecules are not fixed together in any particular way. But it is also similar to a solid because it has a definite volume.

The molecules of a liquid are often attracted to the molecules of other substances. And this attraction is greater than the attraction between neighbouring molecules of the liquid. This is why liquids will rise up a narrow tube. It is called *capillary action*. Water also has a 'skin' called *surface tension*. This is why the pond-skater (above) can walk on the surface.

Gases

Gases behave quite differently from solids and liquids. They are the lightest and most movable form of matter. Any substance on Earth can be turned into a gas if it is heated above its boiling point. Iron becomes a gas if it is heated to about 2900°C. The temperature of the Sun is so high that all the matter in it is in the form of a gas.

Every gas consists of molecules flying about and colliding with each other. The pressure of a mass doubles if its volume is halved (above). But the temperature must remain constant.

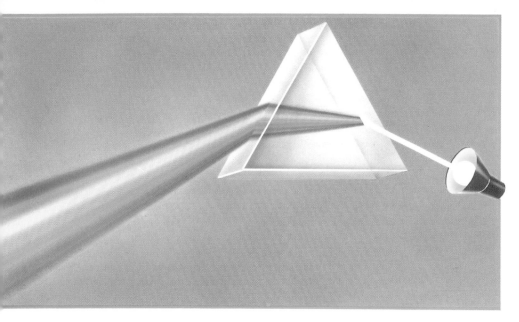

The first man to study light and tell people how it worked was Isaac Newton. In 1665, the great scientist shone a beam of light through a glass *prism,* shaped like the one on the left. He found that the light that came out of the prism had been broken up into all the colours of the rainbow. Newton had discovered that ordinary white light is made up of all the rainbow colours added together. We see a band of colours because our eyes see different wavelengths of light as different colours. Each colour has its own wavelength.

Light and Colour

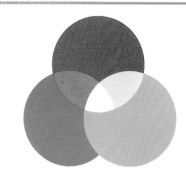

MIXING LIGHT
The three primary colours of light are red, green and blue. Any other colour can be made by mixing these colours. When red, green and blue lights are mixed, the result is white light.

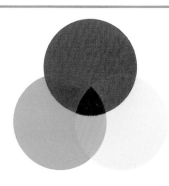

MIXING PAINTS
When paints, inks or dyes are mixed, the basic colours are cyan blue, magenta red and yellow. Cyan and yellow give green. If the three basic colours are mixed, the result is black.

Without light, all life on Earth would come to an end because all the plants and trees would die. People have always realized how important light is, so they tried to find out what it was. Some thought it was made up of tiny particles, others thought it was a series of waves. Today, scientists think that light is neither completely a wave nor completely a stream of particles. It is a cross between the two. But they are still not quite sure what light really is. They do know that light waves are *electromagnetic,* just like radio waves and X-rays.

Radio waves can be kilometres long. Light waves are very short – about five-hundred-thousandths of a centimetre long. This wavelength is important because it limits the size of things we can see through a microscope. If we look at anything about the size of the wavelength of light through a powerful microscope, it is fuzzy.

Invisible Light
Different kinds of light can be seen by different animals. Most humans see all the colours from red through orange, yellow, green, blue to violet.

More than a hundred years ago, scientists tried to find out about the spectrum colours by putting a thermometer in each colour coming from a prism. It was found that as the thermometer was moved from violet to the red end, the temperature increased slightly. But, even more surprising, when the thermometer was placed beyond the red, where there was no visible light, the temperature

was even hotter. There is a hot, invisible radiation just below the red. This radiation is called *infrared* radiation (*infra* means below). Some animals such as the pit viper can actually 'see' these infrared rays, which are really heat rays.

At the other end of the colour spectrum are other beams of 'light' that we cannot see. They are just above the violet, so they are called 'ultraviolet'. Bees can see ultraviolet light although humans cannot.

Light travels in a straight line at a speed of about 300,000km per second. But there are ways of making light change direction. One way is to bounce it off the surface of something. This is called *reflection*. We can see the Moon and the other planets because they reflect the Sun's light. They have no light of their own.

Seems Straight

Place a coin in a cup and move your head back until the coin is just no longer visible. Now, keeping your head steady, pour some water into the cup. Hey presto! The coin appears. This magic is caused by *refraction*. Refraction causes a light beam to bend as it passes from one substance to another. When the light beam from the coin leaves the water and enters the air, it bends so that you can see the coin. The coin looks as though it is in the position at the end of the dotted line in the diagram below. The amount by which light is refracted depends on two things: the angle at which the light beam strikes the second material, and the speed at which the light is travelling. If the light beam goes straight from one substance to another at right angles there is no refraction. If you put the coin in the cup and look straight down on it as you pour in the water, the coin doesn't appear to move. Light travels at its fastest in a vacuum (empty space). In air it travels almost as fast. But in water and glass, light slows down. In fact, in going through some kinds of glass, light travels at only about half its speed in a vacuum – 300,000 km per second.

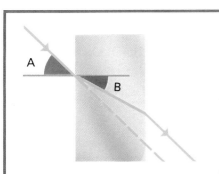

When light passes through a piece of glass it is *refracted*. Angle A is called the *angle of incidence*. Angle B is the *angle of refraction* (the angle by which the beam bends).

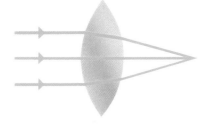

Light is bent in *lenses*. A lens shaped like the one above (convex) brings light rays together at a point called the *focal point*. A magnifying glass is a *convex lens*.

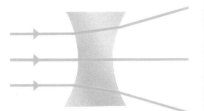

Concave lenses like the one above make light rays spread out. If you look through one, things look smaller. Lenses of this kind are nearly always used with other lenses.

Very Special Light

The laser is one of the most important inventions of the 20th century. A laser beam is a beam of very pure light. We have seen that ordinary light is made up of all the colours of the rainbow. Each colour has a different wavelength. A laser beam has waves that are all the same. The waves rise and fall in step. This makes the laser's narrow beam very powerful. Because of the laser's power and accuracy, it is being used for more and more tasks. It can drill a tiny hole in a diamond, slice through steel plates, help in delicate surgical operations and carry thousands of telephone messages through fine fibres of glass.

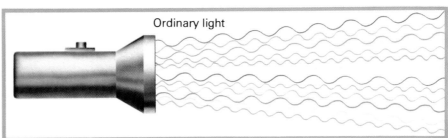

Ordinary light

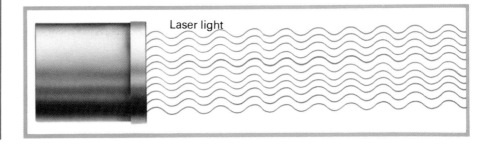

Laser light

The Force of Gravity

An astronaut, hundreds of miles above the Earth, is weightless because he is so far from the Earth's gravitational centre. He feels he is floating and not moving, but both he and his spaceship are travelling at about 30,000 km per hour. The pull of gravity holds him in orbit around the Earth.

Everything in Earth is pulled downwards by a strange force called gravity. The pull of gravity is always towards the centre of the Earth. A stone dropped from someone's hand in England falls to the ground in the same way it would fall in New Zealand on the opposite side of the world. Both stones fall towards the centre of the Earth. And gravity isn't a force that happens only on Earth. Everything in the universe is attracted towards everything else. It is only because the Earth is so big and so close to us that we notice gravity here. The more massive a body, the more material in it, the greater its gravitational pull on other bodies.

The Sun is much more massive than the Earth and all the other planets put together. So the Sun's enormous gravitational pull holds all the planets in place as they circle their big parent body. It is incredible to think that our mighty Earth, speeding along at 30 km per second, is held in its orbit by this invisible bond. In exactly the same way, Earth's gravity holds the Moon in place in its monthly journey around us.

Gravity decreases with distance from the Earth and the same object weighs less and less.

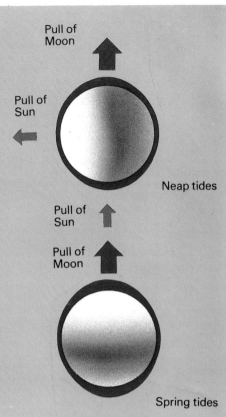

The Tides

Although the Moon's gravity is much less than the Earth's, it still affects us. Tides are caused mainly by the gravitational pull of the Moon, and, to a lesser extent, by the pull of the Sun. When the Moon is overhead, the oceans' waters are drawn towards it, causing a bulge, which is balanced by another bulge on the opposite side of the Earth. High tides are called *spring* tides. They happen when the Earth, Moon and Sun are in a straight line (see diagram). The combined gravitational pull of the Moon and the Sun makes high tides even higher and low tides even lower. The smallest tides – called *neap* tides – happen when the pull of the Moon is at right angles to that of the Sun. Spring tides happen about twice a month, about the time of the full moon and the new moon. Neap tides happen around the first and last quarters of the moon.

Tides occur twice every 24 hours 50 minutes, the time taken for one complete orbit of the Moon around the Earth.

Pull of Moon

Pull of Sun

Neap tides

Pull of Sun

Pull of Moon

Spring tides

The great Italian 16th century scientist Galileo was the first to prove that all objects fall to the ground at the same speed. People knew that a cannon ball falls faster than a feather. But Galileo proved that this was because the feather was slowed down by air resistance. On the Moon, where there is no air, the cannon ball and the feather fall at exactly the same rate.

Losing Gravity

The force of gravity grows less and less the further apart bodies are. When people go up in a spaceship the pull of Earth gravity gets less the higher they go. After a while, the Earth's pull is so small the astronauts do not notice it. They are weightless and live in a strange floating state where there is no 'up' or 'down'.

But what happens if the spaceship goes further and gets close to the Moon? Then the astronauts and their ship begin to come into the pull of the Moon's gravity. With no rockets firing, the spaceship will be pulled faster and faster towards the Moon. If the astronauts land on the Moon they find they can do things they cannot do on Earth. They can lift rocks six times as heavy. Even in their bulky spacesuits they can jump much higher. This is because the gravity of the Moon is only a sixth of Earth gravity. The Moon has only a sixth of the mass of our Earth. If an astronaut who weighed 65 kg on Earth weighed himself on the Moon, the scales would show a weight of only 11 kg. On the other hand, if people ever reach the giant planet Jupiter they will find things much more difficult. If you can jump a height of one metre on Earth, you could only jump 28 cm on Jupiter. And if it were possible to stand on the surface of the Sun, you could not even jump to the height of 3 cm!

A World of Atoms

All substances that exist – human beings, animals, plants, wood, rocks, air, metals, water – are made up of matter. Wood is solid matter; water is liquid matter; and air is gaseous matter.

The smallest piece of a substance that is still recognizable as that substance is called a molecule. The molecule in turn is made up of a number of atoms. Different substances are made up of different kinds of atoms.

The simplest substances are those whose molecules are made up of just one kind of atom. They are called the chemical elements and can be regarded as the building blocks of matter. The metals iron, copper and gold are elements. So are carbon and oxygen.

Other substances have molecules made up of combinations of different atoms. They are called compounds. Atoms of iron, for example, combine with atoms of oxygen to form the compound iron oxide, or rust.

It was once thought that atoms were the smallest particles of matter that could exist – 100 million atoms, side by side, measure only 1 centimetre! But we now know that atoms are made up of even smallest particles and we can even split them.

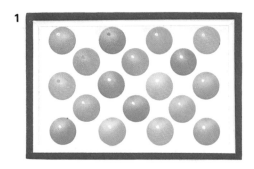

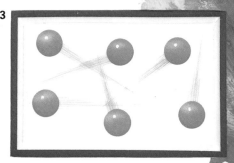

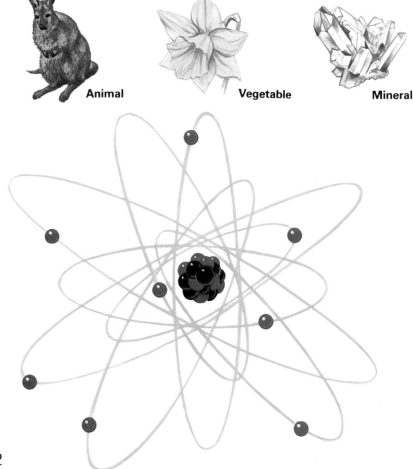

Animal   **Vegetable**   **Mineral**

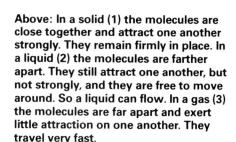

Above: In a solid (1) the molecules are close together and attract one another strongly. They remain firmly in place. In a liquid (2) the molecules are farther apart. They still attract one another, but not strongly, and they are free to move around. So a liquid can flow. In a gas (3) the molecules are far apart and exert little attraction on one another. They travel very fast.

Left: All things on Earth, be they animal, vegetable or mineral, are made up of millions upon millions of atoms. Every atom is constructed in a similar way. The main part is the nucleus. This is made up of tiny particles called protons and neutrons. Around the nucleus circle a number of even tinier particles called electrons. There are as many electrons as there are protons. The protons have a positive electric charge and the electrons have a negative charge. So the atom as a whole is electrically neutral.

Below: The menacing cloud from an atomic-bomb explosion. An atomic explosion has many thousand times the destructive force of an ordinary explosion. It also produces deadly radiation and fallout. Fallout is dangerous radioactive dust carried by winds and falls far away from the site of the explosion.

Below: Energy is released when atoms split, or undergo fission. A uranium atom may undergo fission when it is bombarded by a neutron. It splits into two, releasing energy as light, heat and radiation. Two or more neutrons are also produced in the process. These neutrons may in turn go on to cause fission in other atoms, causing what is called a chain reaction. The energy released when a chain reaction occurs is enormous.

Bottom: The chain reaction is a useful source of power when it can be controlled. This is done in a nuclear reactor. In a reactor, the core contains the uranium 'fuel'. The chain reaction is controlled by means of control rods. A liquid or gas coolant circulates through the core and extracts heat. It gives up this heat to water in a heat exchanger. The steam produced then goes to turbine generating machinery.

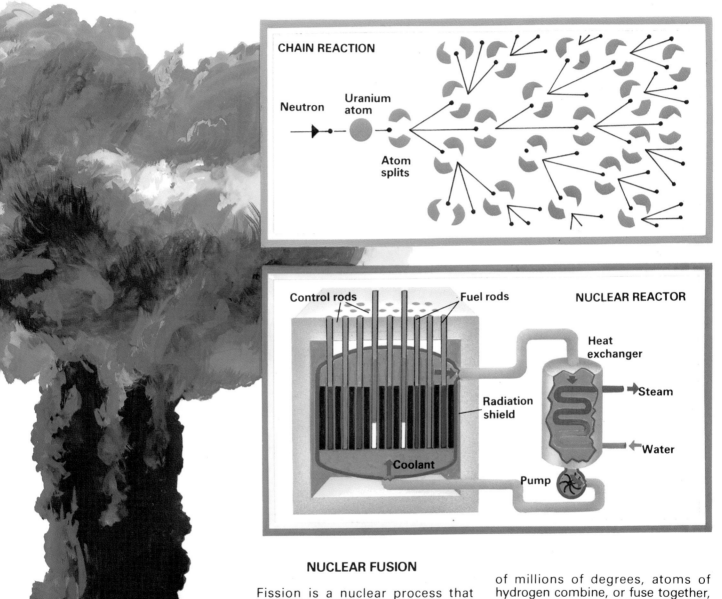

NUCLEAR FUSION

Fission is a nuclear process that occurs when very heavy atoms, such as uranium, split. The opposite kind of process can also occur. Very light atoms can combine to form heavier ones. This process is called fusion. Fusion also releases enormous amounts of energy.

It is in fact fusion that provides the energy to make the Sun and the stars shine. Inside the Sun, at temperatures of millions of degrees, atoms of hydrogen combine, or fuse together, to form atoms of helium.

Scientists on Earth have imitated this process and produced the hydrogen bomb, the most terrible weapon of all. They are now trying to find ways of controlling fusion to produce useful power. They are trying to do this in two ways – with powerful magnetic machines called tokamaks, and with lasers.

Energy and Power

Oil drill pipe

Oil rig

Gas

Oil

Wa

Warm swamps covered many regions of the Earth some 300 million years ago (main picture). In them grew huge ferns and horsetails. When these plants died, they fell into the swamp and began to decay. Over the years the remains dried and hardened into coal, now found sandwiched between the rock layers (inset above). The organisms that lived in ancient seas also died and decayed, and we find their remains today as oil and natural gas, trapped in the rock layers (inset below).

We could not live the way we do today without a plentiful supply of energy. Most of the energy we use comes from oil, coal and natural gas. These are known as fossil fuels because they are the remains of organisms – plants and animals – that once lived. And they are burned to release their energy.

Most oil, or petroleum, is made into fuels that are burned in engines, to power cars, trucks, locomotives and aeroplanes. These fuels include petrol, kerosene and diesel oil. Most coal is burned in power stations to produce electricity. The heat from the burning coal heats water in a boiler into steam. The steam then spins a turbine, which in turn spins a generator to make electricity. Electricity is a very convenient way of 'carrying' energy from place to place.

Some power stations use another kind of 'fuel' to produce heat for the boilers. This is nuclear fuel, such as uranium. Under certain conditions uranium atoms can be made to

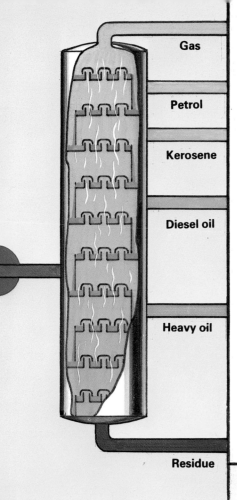

Gas

Petrol

Kerosene

Diesel oil

Heavy oil

Residue

split, and this releases large amount of heat. Nuclear power is an important energy source.

Alternative Energy Sources

Supplies of fossil fuels and uranium are obtained from the ground. Eventually these supplies will run out. Then we must find alternative sources of energy. We are already using one – flowing water. We harness this power in hydro-electric ('water-electric') schemes. The water spins water turbines, which drive the electricity generators.

Schemes to harness other natural energy sources are also well under way. Engineers are building huge wind turbines, wave-power devices and solar 'power towers'.

Left: Before it can be used, crude oil must be refined, or processed, in an oil refinery. The first stage is distillation, which takes place in this kind of tower. Oil vapour passes through the tower, and the various substances it contains separate out into various parts, or fractions.

Below: Some regions of the world are blessed with plenty of sunshine, a 'free' source of energy waiting to be tapped. This can be done with a solar power tower. Large numbers of mirrors reflect sunshine onto a boiler at the top of a tower. This heats water in the boiler into steam.

Heat – Molecules in Motion

Centre of the Sun
15,000,000°C

Surface of the Sun
5500°C

Iron melts
1540°C

Sunlit side of Mercury
375°C

Paper catches fire
284°C

Water boils
100°C

Hottest shade temperature
on Earth 57.7°C

Water freezes
0°C

Coldest temperature on Earth
−88.3°C

Air becomes liquid at about
−200°C

Absolute Zero
−273.16°C

What is heat? Scientists say it is a form of energy – the energy of moving atoms and molecules, that everything is made up of. Atoms and molecules are always on the move, and the heat of anything is simply a measure of how fast they are moving. The faster they move, the hotter a body is.

We measure heat with *thermometers*. Water boils when the thermometer shows 100 on the Centigrade scale (100°C); it freezes at 0°C. Our bodies use the food we eat as fuel to keep our temperature at about 37°C. But temperature and heat are not quite the same thing. If we put two pots on the stove, one full of water, the other with very little water, it will take much longer for the full pot to boil. This means that much more *heat* has to be put into the full pot to get both pots to 100°C.

Heat passes from one place to another in three different ways. They are called *convection, radiation* and *conduction*.

Convection carries heat by circulating it in *convection currents*. A room heater, for example, warms the air around it. This heated air expands and rises and is replaced by cooler air. Then the new cooler air is heated and rises. This means that a constant current of air carries heat all over the room. Convection currents also occur in liquids (right).

With radiation, heat travels through empty space. When something gets hot, its moving atoms and molecules make invisible waves of radiant energy. These waves are also called *infra-red rays*. The heat that reaches us from the Sun has travelled by radiation rays at the speed of light. Heat waves and light waves are exactly the same except for their different wavelengths.

Conduction is the movement of heat through a material or from one body to another if the bodies are touching. If we place one end of a metal spoon in boiling water, the handle of the spoon soon becomes too hot to hold. The heat from the water has travelled up the spoon by conduction. Some materials such as metals are good conductors – they conduct heat easily; other substances such as wood are bad conductors.

Left: An example of the tremendous range of temperatures experienced in the universe.

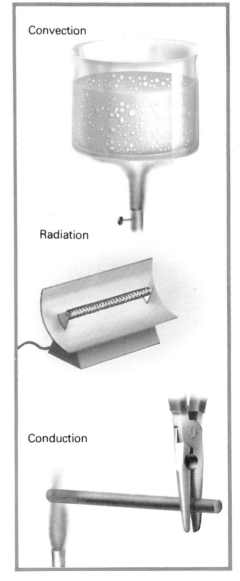

Convection

Radiation

Conduction

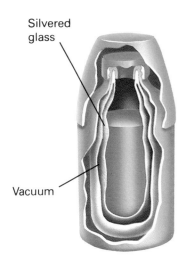

Silvered glass

Vacuum

Vacuum flasks keep things hot or cold for a long time. There is a vacuum between the double walls of the flask to stop heat loss by conduction. The container is also silvered to help stop loss of heat by radiation.

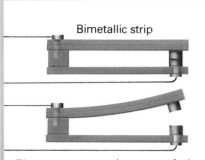

Bimetallic strip

Thermostats make use of the fact that some substances expand and contract more than others when they are heated. They are used in heating systems, cookers and irons to switch the heat on when the temperature falls too low, and to switch it off again when the required temperature is reached. They are also used in refrigerators.

Many thermostats have a *bimetallic strip* made of two different metals such as brass and iron fastened together. As the temperature rises, the brass expands more than the iron. This makes the strip bend upwards. The electrical contact is broken and the heating current stops flowing. As the bimetallic strip cools down again the brass contracts until the two metals are the same size once more. The contact is made and the heating current flows once more.

Hot and Cold

Steel begins to melt at a temperature of about 1500°C, but this is very chilly compared to the heat of the Sun. Inside the Sun the temperature is about 15 million degrees. Other stars are much hotter still. There appears to be no limit to how hot it can get.

Cold is different. The coldest place on Earth is a chilly −88°C (88 degrees below zero). But the thermometer would have to drop to −183°C before the air started to freeze. At −273°C, *absolute zero* is reached. At this temperature everything would be frozen solid. Nothing would move. Even the atoms would stop moving. But it is not possible to reach this temperature.

Nearly everything grows bigger when it is heated. If you place a thermometer in hot water, the atoms in the mercury move faster and faster and take up more space. The mercury expands and moves up the thermometer's stem.

A fire-fighter wears a special suit so that he can walk through flames and remain unharmed. The suit is made of asbestos, a substance that is a very poor conductor of heat. The silvery surface of the suit reflects heat away.

Chemical Reactions

Chemistry is the study of substances. It looks at what they are made of and how they split up or join together with other substances. Everything around us is made of chemicals. The water we drink, the salt and sugar we eat are chemicals. So are the proteins that make up most of all plants and animals.

There are just over a hundred basic chemicals called *elements*. Everything is made up of these. Iron, oxygen, carbon, gold and silver are all elements. And elements are made up of tiny atoms. Each element has its own kind of atom that is different from the atoms of all the other elements. When the atoms of two or more different elements join together, they form a chemical *compound*. Water is a compound of the elements of hydrogen and oxygen. Two atoms of hydrogen join with one atom of oxygen to make a *molecule* of water.

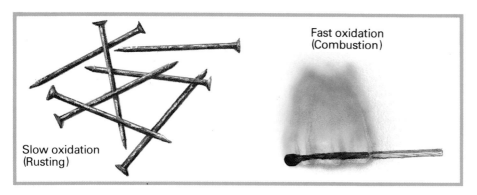

Fast oxidation
(Combustion)

Slow oxidation
(Rusting)

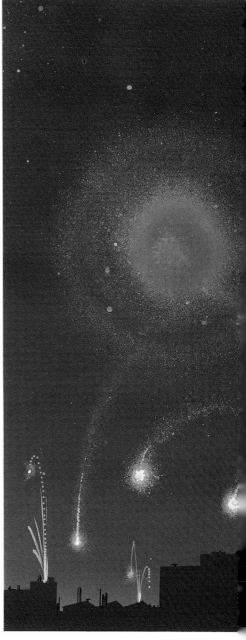

Some compounds are very complicated. Each molecule of sugar, for example, contains 22 hydrogen atoms, 11 oxygen atoms and 12 carbon atoms. Sugar, starch and alcohol all have molecules that contain hydrogen, oxygen and carbon, but in different proportions. It is the different proportions that make the three substances different.

Chemists use symbols to name substances. Chemical formulas show the elements that make up the substances. The symbol for the element hydrogen is H; for oxygen it is O. The formula for water is H_2O.

Vast quantities of chemicals are used in the modern world. Soaps and detergents, dyes and acids, polishes, artificial fibres and explosives – all these things and thousands more are products of the vast chemical industry.

When something burns very quickly indeed, we say it 'explodes'. The exploding force in fireworks (above) comes from the rapid burning of gunpowder. Gunpowder is a mixture of sulphur, saltpetre and charcoal. When an explosion happens, a quite small quantity of explosive such as gunpowder burns in a flash and turns into a large amount of hot gas. It is this expanding gas that sends rockets into the air. The brilliant colours of fireworks comes from metallic salts that are added. Calcium salts give a red colour; sodium, yellow; barium, green; and copper, blue and green.

Spinneret

Nylon threads

Man-made fibres are made from polymers. In making nylon, the polymer is melted and then forced through fine holes to make nylon threads. As the nylon comes through the holes it cools and hardens. The fine threads are often twisted together to make a stronger thread (see left). The picture above shows the nylon being forced through the holes in a *spinneret*.

Substances that are made up of long chains of carbon atoms are often called *polymers*. Cotton is a natural polymer because the fibres of cotton are made up of a polymer called *cellulose*. Cellulose is a compound with long chains of carbon atoms. Nowadays, chemists make artificial **polymers. For example, molecules of the gas ethylene join together in a long chain to make polyethylene – the plastic we call Polythene (see above). There are many different plastics that rely on the joining together of carbon atoms. Plastics have countless uses.**

Sodium hydroxide Hydrochloric acid Sodium chloride Water

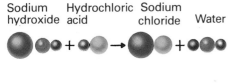

Acids turn litmus paper red. *Bases* turn litmus paper blue. Acids and bases neutralize each other – they cancel each other out. Bases that dissolve in water are called *alkalis*. When a base neutralizes an acid it makes salt and water only. If we take a solution of sodium hydroxide (a base) and add it to hydrochloric acid in the right quantities, the result is neutral. We are left with sodium chloride (table salt) and water (see above).

Slow and Fast Burning

Oxygen is the most plentiful of all the elements in nature. Although it is a gas we cannot see, it accounts for about half the weight of most rocks and minerals. A fifth of the air we breathe is oxygen, and nearly all living things need it.

Oxygen is a very active chemical. It combines with many other chemical elements to make a very large number of compounds. These compounds are called *oxides*. The process in which they are made is called *oxidation*. Slow oxidation happens when iron is in damp air. This produces *iron oxide*, which we call rust. When oxygen and another element are combined rapidly, light and heat are given off. We call fast oxidation *combustion*, or burning.

Magnets

A magnet is any piece of metal that will attract or pull towards itself iron, steel or a few other metals. Magnets can be of different sizes and shapes, and they can be strong or weak. The ends of magnets are called their *poles*. One end is called the *north-seeking pole* (N); the other is the *south-seeking pole* (S).

Magnets are very important. They are used every day in telephones and in the loudspeakers of television sets and radios. And they are a vital part of the big generators that make our electricity.

The magnet on the right is called a *horseshoe magnet*. If we hang chains of pins from it, each pin becomes a small magnet; each with its own north and south poles.

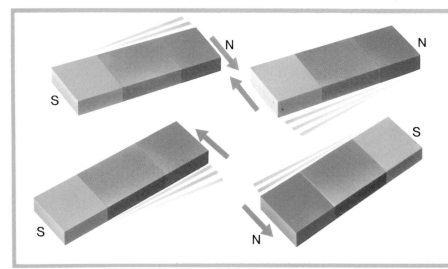

The magnets on the left are called bar magnets. If we place the south pole of one magnet near the north pole of another, the magnets will be attracted to each other. If we place the north pole of one near the north pole of another, they will push each other apart. We say that unlike poles attract and like poles repel. All magnets have more magnetic pull at their ends than at their middle.

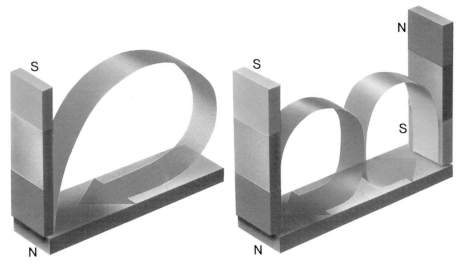

There are several ways of making magnets. One way is to stroke a permanent magnet across the metal to be magnetized, usually a piece of iron. (Soft iron is easier to magnetize than hard steel.) The iron must be stroked in one direction only, as shown in the pictures on the left.

A weak magnet can also be made by placing the iron in line with the Earth's magnetic field and hammering it. An electric current flowing in a coil around the metal will also magnetize it.

Magnets can be made to lose their magnetism by hammering them or by heating them in a flame.

Magnetic Fields

Every magnet has an invisible *magnetic field* going through it and around it. The field around a bar magnet can be seen if we lay a sheet of paper over the magnet and sprinkle iron filings on the paper. When the paper is tapped, the iron filings will move into lines, called *lines of force,* around the magnet. Most of the lines cluster round the ends of the magnet where the magnetism is strongest.

The magnet on the right is called a *horseshoe magnet.* If we move a small compass around in the horseshoe magnet's field and note the way the compass needle points, we can draw a pattern of lines as in the picture.

The Earth has a weak magnetic field, rather like that of an enormous bar magnet. Compass needles all over the world point north and south because of the Earth's magnetism.

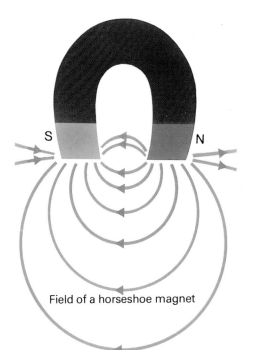
Field of a horseshoe magnet

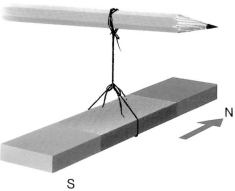

If a bar magnet is suspended as shown above, it will always come to rest pointing in a North–South direction. And always the same end of the magnet points North. A compass (below) is really a small, lightweight magnet. It is pivoted so that it can move freely. The Earth's North pole always attracts the magnet's South pole.

The end of the magnet that points North is called the magnet's *North-seeking pole*.

Compass

The Earth's magnetic field

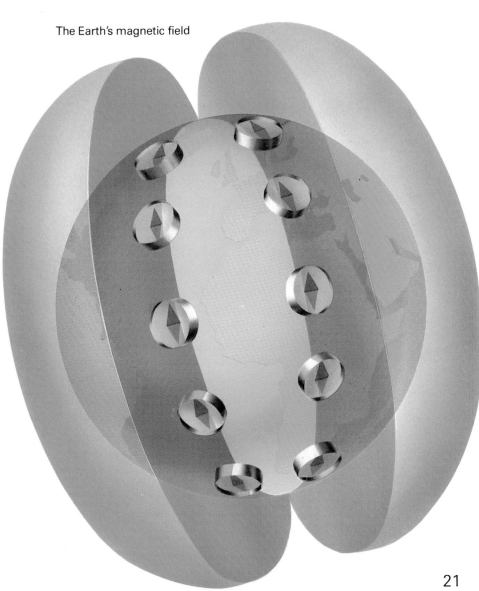

Making Electricity

When ancient people saw lightning flashes in the sky, they thought the gods were angry. They did not know about electricity, but they noticed that some things seemed at times to attract other things. The ancient Greeks knew that if they rubbed a piece of amber with a woollen cloth, straw and dry leaves were attracted to it.

Today, we know that both the lightning and the amber's attraction are forms of electricity. Lightning happens when clouds store up too much electricity. Electric sparks which we call lightning shoot from the clouds to other clouds or to the ground.

An electric current is a movement, or flow, of tiny particles called *electrons*. Electrons are particles of negative electricity that circle around the centre of every atom. In some materials, a few of the electrons are only loosely held to their atoms. They are free to jump from atom to atom. When they do this, an electric current flows. An electric current is started by a battery or electric generator. If the

When the terminals of a battery are connected by a wire, an electric current flows from one terminal to the other. Most metals are good conductors of electricity – especially copper and silver. Wires are usually made of copper. The copper atoms have *free* electrons that can be pushed on to the next atom in the line. Another free electron is pushed from that atom, and so on to the other battery terminal. This is an electric current.

Electricity can be produced by separating two different metals with a solution that conducts electricity. A 'dry' cell is not really dry. It is filled with a damp chemical paste. The positive terminal is a carbon rod. The zinc container is the negative electrode.

An accumulator or battery contains cells made of lead plates in dilute sulphuric acid. Car batteries usually have six 2-volt cells. They are connected in series to give 12 volts.

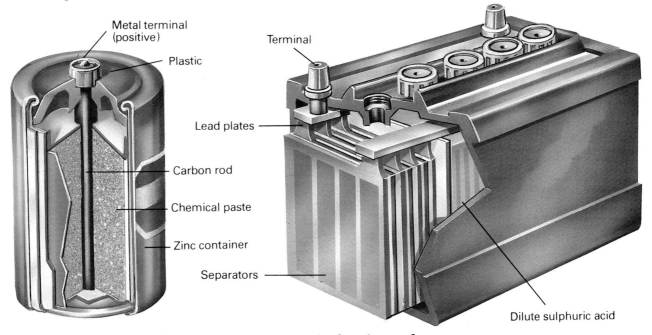

Metal terminal (positive)

Plastic

Terminal

Lead plates

Carbon rod

Chemical paste

Zinc container

Separators

Dilute sulphuric acid

terminals of a battery are connected to each end of a piece of wire, electrons are pushed from the first atom in the line to the next, and so on along the wire – all in a flash of time. Wires which carry electric current are often made of copper. Copper, like most metals, is a good *conductor* of electricity. It has lots of free electrons.

Batteries and Generators

Batteries make electricity by chemical action. The most common kind of battery – the flashlight battery – is really a *dry cell*. When the chemicals in the cell are used up, the cell is dead and is thrown away. A battery is two or more cells working together.

A car battery is different. It is filled with dilute sulphuric acid in which are lead plates. When this kind of battery runs down it can be recharged by connecting it to an electric current. This makes the chemical action go backwards. The electrons are put back where they were and the battery can produce current again.

An electric generator is a machine that turns mechanical energy into electrical energy. The simplest generator is a loop of wire that is turned between the poles of a magnet. When the wire cuts the lines of force between the magnet's poles, an electric current is produced in the wire. This is the principle of the electric generator.

The diagram below shows a very simple electric generator. A loop of wire is turned between the poles of a permanent magnet. As the wire cuts the lines of magnetic force between the magnet's poles, an electric current is produced in the wire. The current is taken from the wire loop through carbon brushes that rub against metal rings. Large generators have thousands of loops of wire and produce a very large, steady current.

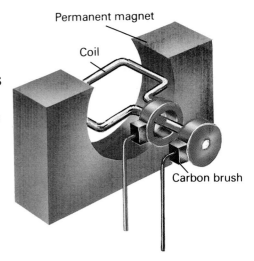

Permanent magnet

Coil

Carbon brush

23

Putting Electricity to Work

When an electric current goes through the fine coiled wire *filament* inside a light bulb, the filament gets hot and glows with light. The filament is made of tungsten, a metal that does not melt easily when it is hot. The bulb has no air in it and has other gases to help stop the filament burning out.

Electricity is the most useful form of energy. It can be taken easily by cables to our homes, factories and offices and there used to produce light and heat or run machines.

The electricity we use is produced at power stations by large generators. These are machines that are turned by power from coal or oil to make electricity. Electricity flows along wires as a current. A current of electricity must have a completely unbroken path. If we could follow a current from the generator, it would travel across country through heavy overhead copper wires and along underground cables to our house. There it would go through a meter that would show how much current went through it; through fuses, to an electric light bulb. After the current has passed through the bulb and produced light, it goes all the way back through a separate wire to the generator in the power station. All this happens in a flash.

Most electricity is used to make things move. What do vacuum cleaners, food mixers and tape recorders have in common? They all have *electric motors* inside them to make things go round (see opposite page).

Some of the most powerful electric motors are used to drive electric trains. The electricity can be carried to the train's motors in different ways. Some railways have overhead wires above the track. A metal bar reaches up from the train and slides along the wire to collect the electric current. This is called a *pantograph*. Other trains get their power from a third rail placed beside the track.

HOW AN ELECTRIC MOTOR WORKS

The diagrams show how a simple motor works. When a current flows through the coil, a magnetic field is set up. The coil then has a north pole and a south pole as shown by the 'ghost' magnet drawn as though it were inside the coil. Permanent magnets give a magnetic field in which the coil turns. Forces of attraction and repulsion between the fields make the coil turn. As the coil turns *carbon brushes* rub against separate *commutator* segments to carry current to the coil as shown. When the poles of the coil are almost in line with the poles of the permanent magnet, the brushes are almost at the end of the commutator segments (1). But the moving coil cannot stop and carries on past this point. At the same time the commutator reverses the current flowing through the coil and in doing so reverses the poles of the coil (2). (This is shown in the diagram by the ghost magnet. The end with the black dot has changed from blue to red.) Forces of attraction and repulsion between the coil and the permanent magnet keep the coil turning (3) until the commutator changes the poles again (4). In this way the coil, or motor, keeps turning.

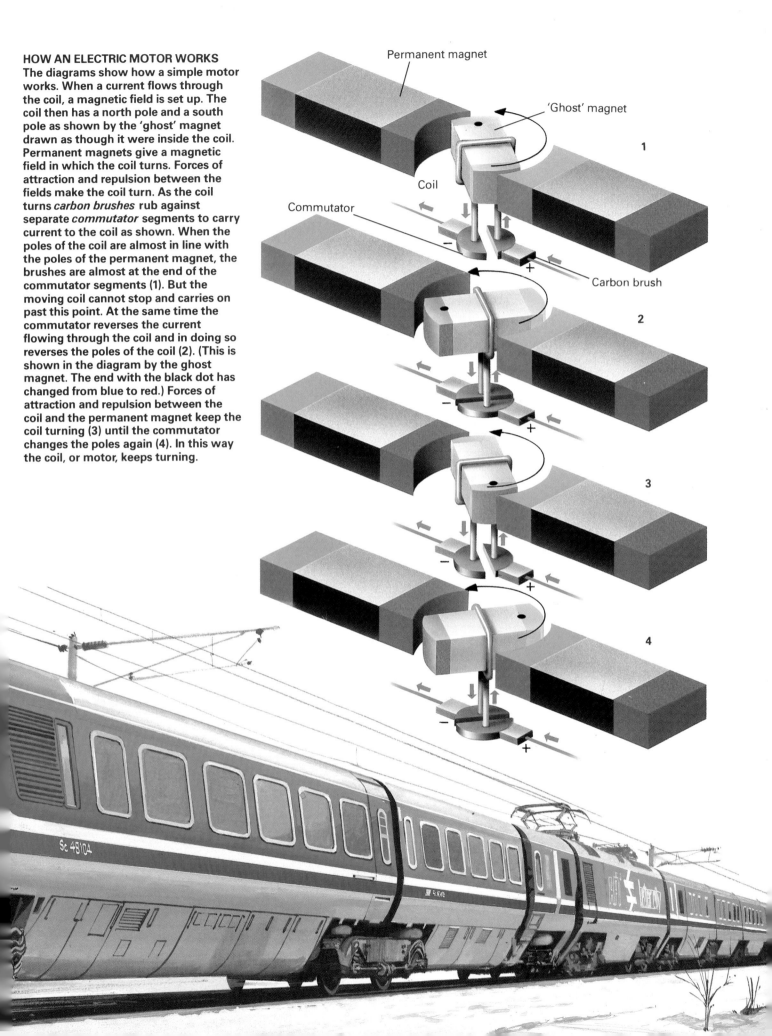

Permanent magnet

'Ghost' magnet

Coil

Commutator

Carbon brush

1

2

3

4

Sc 45104

Great Inventions

The story of civilization can be traced in the inventions that Man has made. Among the early inventions of greatest importance were metal smelting, in the 4000s BC; the wheel and the plough, in the 3000s BC; and the harnessing of water power, in Roman times. But the pace of invention was slow until the 1400s, the time of the Renaissance, or 'rebirth of learning'.

Hot air balloon, 1783

The wheel was invented about 3000 BC

1450	**Printing Press** Johannes Gutenberg, Germany
1590	**Compound Microscope** Zacharias Janssen, the Netherlands
1608/9	**Refracting Telescope** Hans Lippershey, the Netherlands, and Galileo Galilei, Italy
1668	**Reflecting Telescope** Isaac Newton, Britain
1698	**Steam Pump** Thomas Savery, Britain
1712	**Beam Engine** Thomas Newcomen, Britain
1733	**Flying Shuttle** John Kay, Britain
1767	**Spinning Jenny** James Hargreaves, Britain
1780s	**Improved Steam Engine** James Watt, Britain
1783	**Hot-air Balloon** Montgolfier Brothers, France
1785	**Power Loom** Edmund Cartwright, Britain
1792	**Cotton Gin** Eli Whitney, United States
1800	**Electric Battery** Allessandro Volta, Italy
1800	**Lathe** Henry Maudslay, Britain
1804	**Steam Locomotive** Richard Trevithick, Britain
1815	**Safety Lamp** Humphry Davy, Britain
1815	**Stethoscope** René T. H. Laënec, France
1836	**Revolver** Samuel Colt, United States
1837	**Telegraph** William Cooke and Charles Wheatstone, Britain; Samuel Morse, United States
1839	**Steam Hammer** James Nasmyth, Britain
1845	**Sewing Machine** Elias Howe, United States
1856	**Bessemer Process** Henry Bessemer, Britain
1867	**Dynamite** Alfred Nobel, Sweden
1872	**Typewriter** Christopher L. Scholes, United States
1876	**Telephone** Alexander Graham Bell, United States
1877	**Phonograph (Gramophone)** Thomas Alva Edison, United States
1878	**Cathode-Ray Tube** William Crookes, Britain
1878/9	**Electric Lamp** Joseph Swan, Britain, and Thomas Alva Edison, United States
1880s	**Machine Gun** Hiram Stevens Maxim, United States
1884	**Steam Turbine** Charles Algernon Parsons, Britain
1885	**Petrol Engine** Karl Benz and Gottlieb Daimler, Germany
1888	**Pneumatic Tyre** John Boyd Dunlop, Britain
1892	**Diesel Engine** Rudolf Diesel, Germany
1895	**Radio** Guglielmo Marconi, Italy
1903	**Powered Aircraft** Wilbur and Orville Wright, United States
1926	**Television** John Logie Baird, Britain, and Vladimir Zworykin, United States
1930	**Jet Engine** Frank Whittle, Britain
1944	**Digital Computer** Howard Aiken, United States
1947	**Polaroid Camera** Edwin H. Land, United States
1955	**Hovercraft** Christopher Cockerell, Britain
1971	**Microprocessor** Intel Corporation, United States

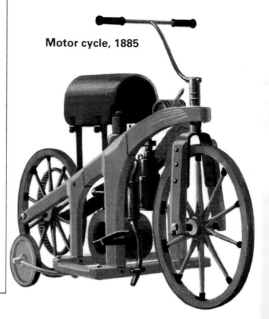

Motor cycle, 1885

The Wright brothers' 'Flyer'

The windmill was invented in Persia about AD 600

Telegraph, 1837

The bowdrill was invented about 50,000 years ago

Early TV tube

Early telephone

Early phonograph

Stephenson's Rocket, 1830

Early Scholes typewriter

Early Colt revolver

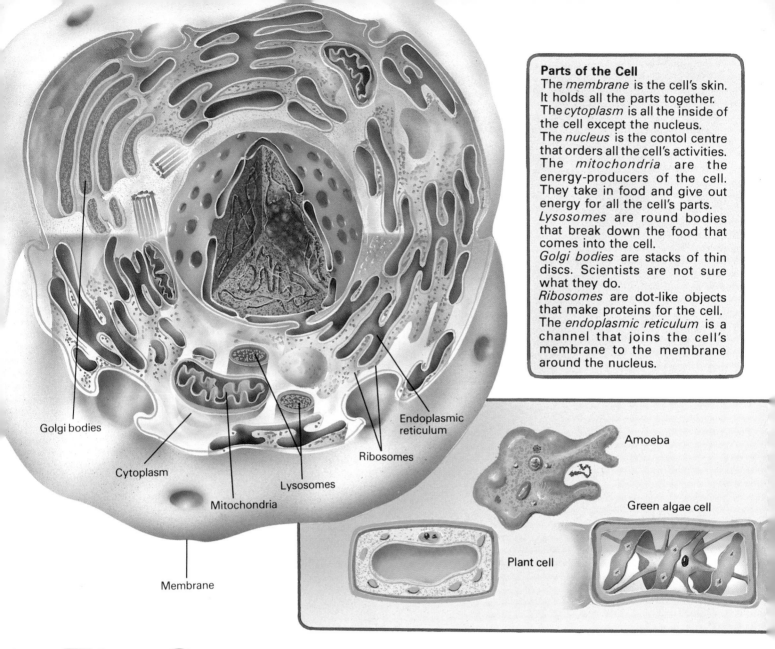

Parts of the Cell
The *membrane* is the cell's skin. It holds all the parts together.
The *cytoplasm* is all the inside of the cell except the nucleus.
The *nucleus* is the contol centre that orders all the cell's activities.
The *mitochondria* are the energy-producers of the cell. They take in food and give out energy for all the cell's parts.
Lysosomes are round bodies that break down the food that comes into the cell.
Golgi bodies are stacks of thin discs. Scientists are not sure what they do.
Ribosomes are dot-like objects that make proteins for the cell.
The *endoplasmic reticulum* is a channel that joins the cell's membrane to the membrane around the nucleus.

Golgi bodies

Cytoplasm

Mitochondria

Lysosomes

Ribosomes

Endoplasmic reticulum

Membrane

Amoeba

Green algae cell

Plant cell

The Science of Life

Our bodies are made up of millions upon millions of tiny cells. All these cells grow from only two cells that join together at conception, when a new life begins. The cells come in all shapes and sizes. Some brain cells are only $\frac{1}{200}$ mm across. Other cells, such as muscle and nerve cells, are long and thin. Nerve cells can be as much as a metre long.

But all cells are similar in some ways. They are all enclosed in a thin membrane. Inside the membrane is the *cytoplasm*. This jelly-like stuff contains several different structures, and each has its own job to do. At the cell's centre is its *nucleus*. The nucleus is the cell's 'brain', controlling everything that the cell does.

The nucleus is the cell's control room. Fine strands called *chromosomes* are scattered inside it. Chromosomes are made up of two kinds of substances – DNA and *proteins*. DNA is a chemical that controls all the things that are passed on from one generation to the next. It rules whether we will have fair or dark hair, blue eyes or brown. DNA does this by controlling the production of other substances called proteins.

Cells at Work

Below you can see some of the different kinds of living cells. *Red blood cells* are those that make our blood look red. They carry oxygen from the lungs all over our bodies. *White blood cells* are those that we need to protect us from disease. *Nerve cells* are shaped as they are so that they can carry messages to different parts of the body. *Lymphocytes* and *phagocytes* are two kinds of cell which 'eat' harmful bacteria in the body. When we cut ourself, bacteria often attack the wound. Then phagocytes come along and attack and surround the bacteria. If the invading bacteria or micro-organisms are still not beaten, the lymphocytes come along and secrete *antibodies* that make the invaders harmless.

Amoebas are tiny creatures that consist of only one cell. All the machinery for life is held inside them. Despite their small size, they are able to move about, feed themselves and reproduce.

Passing On the Information

A new life begins when two cells join to make a new one. This new cell must have in it all the characteristics that a person inherits from his or her parents. The cell must also contain all the information needed to build up a human body.

Each chromosome in the cell's nucleus is a chain of things called *genes.* There may be 1000 of them on each chromosome. The genes govern our hair colour, eye colour and all our other characteristics. The genes are made of DNA. Each DNA molecule is arranged in two spirals linked by chemicals, rather like the rungs of a ladder (see below). There are only four different chemical rungs but they can be arranged in a huge variety of combinations to give all the different characteristics that people have.

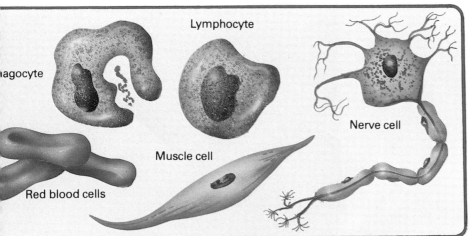

Lymphocyte

Phagocyte

Nerve cell

Muscle cell

Red blood cells

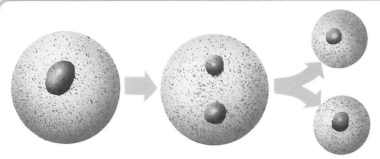

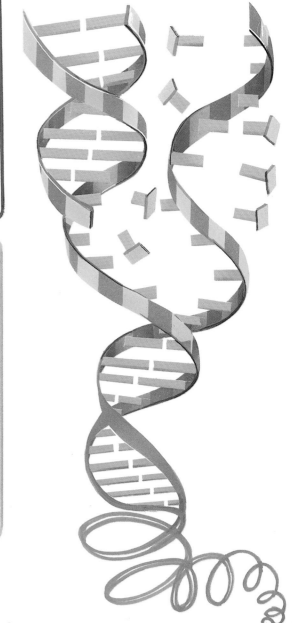

Making New Cells

The only way new tissue can be formed is from the division of cells. The nucleus splits in half to make two identical nuclei, each with a full set of chromosomes. Then the cell itself divides to make two cells.

There is another kind of cell division which takes place in *sex* cells. In this process, the parent sex cell, male or female, divides in such a way that each new cell has only half the number of chromosomes of the parent cell. So when the sex cells meet, each gives a half set of chromosomes to the new cell, which must therefore have a complete set of chromosomes, half from the father and half from the mother.

Science in the Home

Science has played a big part in making our homes comfortable and easy to operate. Even forgetting such things as television sets, radios, refrigerators and food mixers, there are many other ways in which science works for us. Many of the home inventions of the past hundred years are now so much a part of our daily lives that we seldom stop to think about them. The first canned food, for example, went on sale in the 1820s. But it was not until the 1860s that the first can-opener was invented. Before then, people opened cans with a hammer and chisel!

Cleaning and washing used to be hard work, often needing servants armed with mops and brooms. Then science came to our aid. The carpet sweeper was invented in

It is very seldom we have to think about all the wires, pipes and tanks that are hidden behind the walls, under the floors and in the lofts of our homes. Some of them are shown in the picture below. The big tank feeds all the water pipes throughout the house. The smaller tanks are fed from it and are for the hot water system. The hot water boiler on the ground floor may use gas, coal or oil to heat the water. The electricity supply comes in through a main fuse box. You can see how the wires run from a fuse through all the electric sockets in a room back to the fuse box.

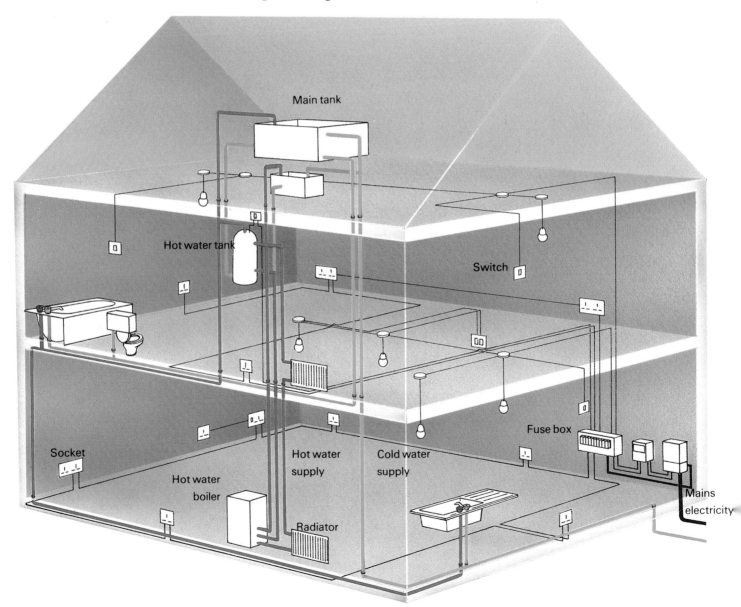

Main tank

Hot water tank

Switch

Socket

Hot water supply

Cold water supply

Fuse box

Hot water boiler

Radiator

Mains electricity

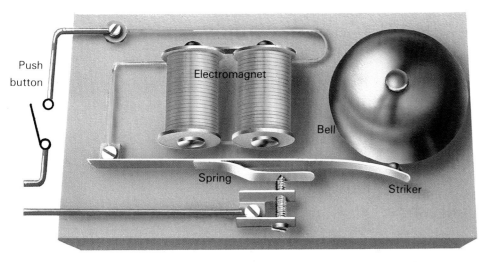

Push button

Electromagnet

Bell

Spring

Striker

When you press the button of an electric bell you close a switch that makes an electric current flow through an electromagnet. This magnetism moves a striker which hits the bell. As the striker moves, it opens the contact that passes current to the electromagnet. There is no magnetism, so a spring pulls the striker back. This closes the contact again and current passes again to the electromagnet. The bell rings and opens the contact again. In this way, the bell keeps on ringing as long as the button is pressed.

1876, soon followed by the hand-cranked vacuum cleaner, worked by bellows. In 1901 an electric motor and an air filter turned it into the vacuum cleaner.

The first washing machines were also worked by turning a handle. By 1914, electric motors were being used. Although detergents were invented as long ago as 1916, it was not until 1945 that they came into general use.

The oil lamp, like the candle, was one of the earliest and most useful inventions. Then came gas in the early 1800s. But gas light was rather poor until the invention of the incandescent mantle in 1885. The mantle was a sleeve of fine cotton soaked in chemicals. This fitted over the gas flame and burned to increase and spread the light. The carbon-filament electric lamp, invented around 1878, was the forerunner of today's tungsten-filament lamp and the fluorescent tube. Many other inventions, big and small, help to make our lives easier; things like safety pins, zip fasteners, sewing machines, safety razors, water closets and non-stick frying pans.

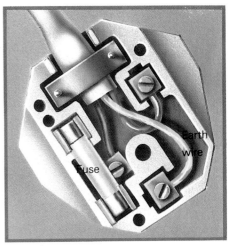

Earth wire

Fuse

Electric plugs (above) should have a fuse inside them for safety. Inside the tube is a thin wire which melts if too much current passes through it. This cuts off the electricity before any damage is done. Without a fuse, an electrical fault could cause the current to rise and cause overheating and start a fire. Fuses are graded in amperes (amps) – an amp is the unit of electric current. The number of amps printed on a fuse is the amount of current that the fuse will allow through to whatever appliance is being used without 'blowing'.

A refrigerator has pipes inside it that contain a cold fluid. This fluid easily changes from a liquid to a vapour. As it goes into the refrigerator it is liquid and is pumped through an evaporator. This lowers the liquid's pressure and it becomes vapour. The change from liquid to vapour makes the vapour cold. This cold vapour flows through pipes inside the refrigerator. After it leaves, it goes to a condenser. This increases its pressure and it changes back to liquid, giving out heat. In this way, heat is taken from inside the refrigerator to the outside.

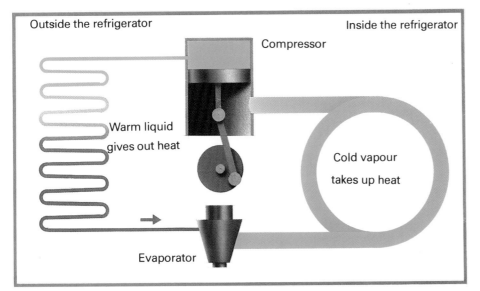

Outside the refrigerator

Inside the refrigerator

Compressor

Warm liquid gives out heat

Cold vapour takes up heat

Evaporator

Science in the Air

The cockpit of a modern airliner is a mass of electronics. A dazzling variety of dials and warning lights face the pilot. They keep him informed as to how all the plane's systems are working, whether he is on course and so on.

As the aircraft approaches an airport an Instrument Landing System guides it in. Ground control supplies the pilot with direction of approach. Aircraft usually start to line up with the runway about 7 to 10 kilometres from the airport; then they follow radio beams until they land. Landing has become more and more automatic, and many aircraft can now land without the pilot touching the controls at all.

Despite all these electronic aids, aircraft still need pilots. In passenger planes, two sets of all essential equipment are carried, in case one fails. But even if both sets fail, the air crew are still there to bring the plane safely to land.

THE ALTIMETER

The pressure altimeter (opposite) tells the pilot how high he is above sea level. In the instrument is a sealed thin metal capsule filled with air. The pressure inside the capsule is always the same. But as the plane goes higher, the air pressure around it grows less. The air in the capsule can then push the thin metal outward. This turns a lever which works a pointer. Pipes connect the altimeter to the air outside the plane.

AEROFOILS

To fly, an aircraft must in some way lift itself off the ground against the pull of the Earth's gravity. This lift is produced by air flowing over the plane's wings. The wings have a special shape called an *aerofoil.* They are curved at the top and flat at the bottom. This means that the air passing over the top of the wing has to travel faster because it has further to go. So the air pressure is less above the wing than below it and the wing is lifted upward.

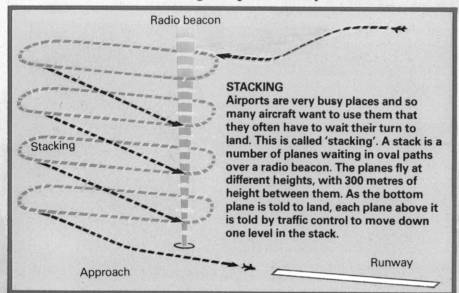

Radio beacon

STACKING

Stacking

Airports are very busy places and so many aircraft want to use them that they often have to wait their turn to land. This is called 'stacking'. A stack is a number of planes waiting in oval paths over a radio beacon. The planes fly at different heights, with 300 metres of height between them. As the bottom plane is told to land, each plane above it is told by traffic control to move down one level in the stack.

Approach

Runway

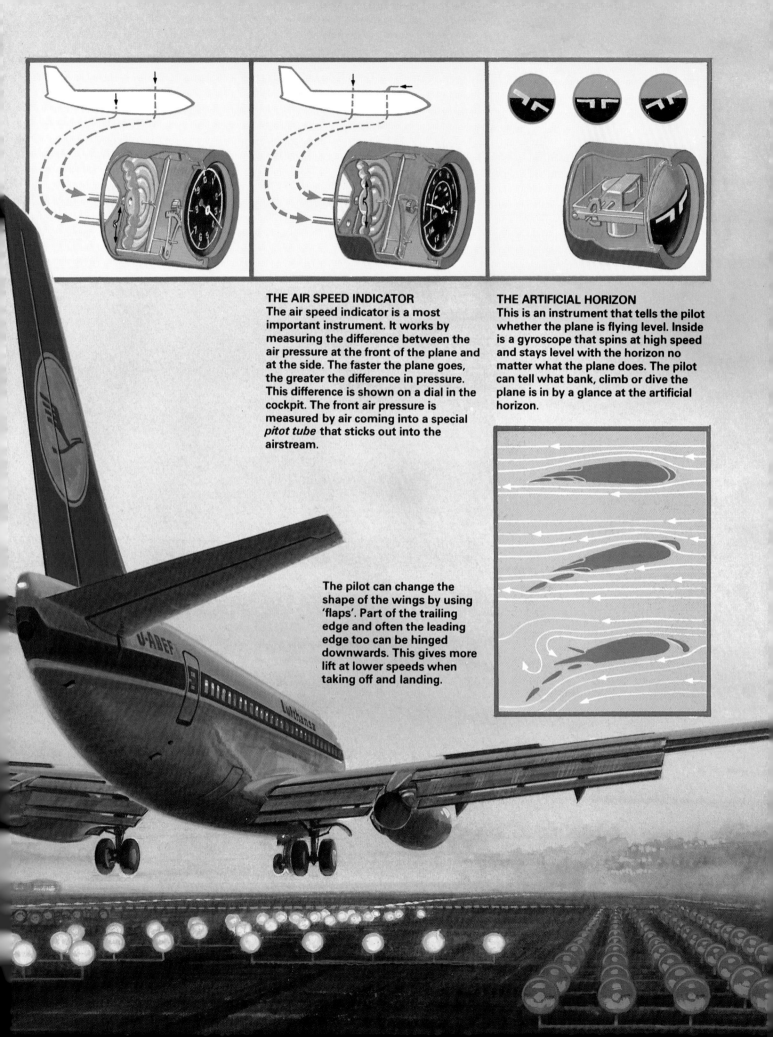

THE AIR SPEED INDICATOR

The air speed indicator is a most important instrument. It works by measuring the difference between the air pressure at the front of the plane and at the side. The faster the plane goes, the greater the difference in pressure. This difference is shown on a dial in the cockpit. The front air pressure is measured by air coming into a special *pitot tube* that sticks out into the airstream.

THE ARTIFICIAL HORIZON

This is an instrument that tells the pilot whether the plane is flying level. Inside is a gyroscope that spins at high speed and stays level with the horizon no matter what the plane does. The pilot can tell what bank, climb or dive the plane is in by a glance at the artificial horizon.

The pilot can change the shape of the wings by using 'flaps'. Part of the trailing edge and often the leading edge too can be hinged downwards. This gives more lift at lower speeds when taking off and landing.

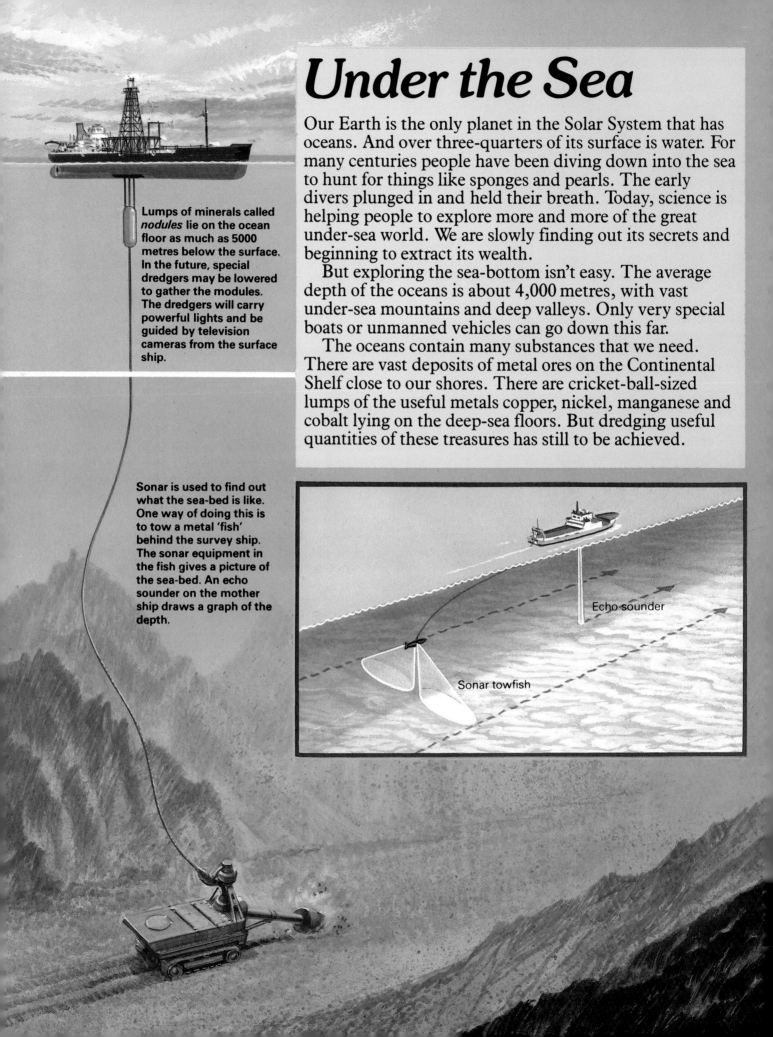

Under the Sea

Our Earth is the only planet in the Solar System that has oceans. And over three-quarters of its surface is water. For many centuries people have been diving down into the sea to hunt for things like sponges and pearls. The early divers plunged in and held their breath. Today, science is helping people to explore more and more of the great under-sea world. We are slowly finding out its secrets and beginning to extract its wealth.

But exploring the sea-bottom isn't easy. The average depth of the oceans is about 4,000 metres, with vast under-sea mountains and deep valleys. Only very special boats or unmanned vehicles can go down this far.

The oceans contain many substances that we need. There are vast deposits of metal ores on the Continental Shelf close to our shores. There are cricket-ball-sized lumps of the useful metals copper, nickel, manganese and cobalt lying on the deep-sea floors. But dredging useful quantities of these treasures has still to be achieved.

Lumps of minerals called *nodules* lie on the ocean floor as much as 5000 metres below the surface. In the future, special dredgers may be lowered to gather the modules. The dredgers will carry powerful lights and be guided by television cameras from the surface ship.

Sonar is used to find out what the sea-bed is like. One way of doing this is to tow a metal 'fish' behind the survey ship. The sonar equipment in the fish gives a picture of the sea-bed. An echo sounder on the mother ship draws a graph of the depth.

Echo sounder

Sonar towfish

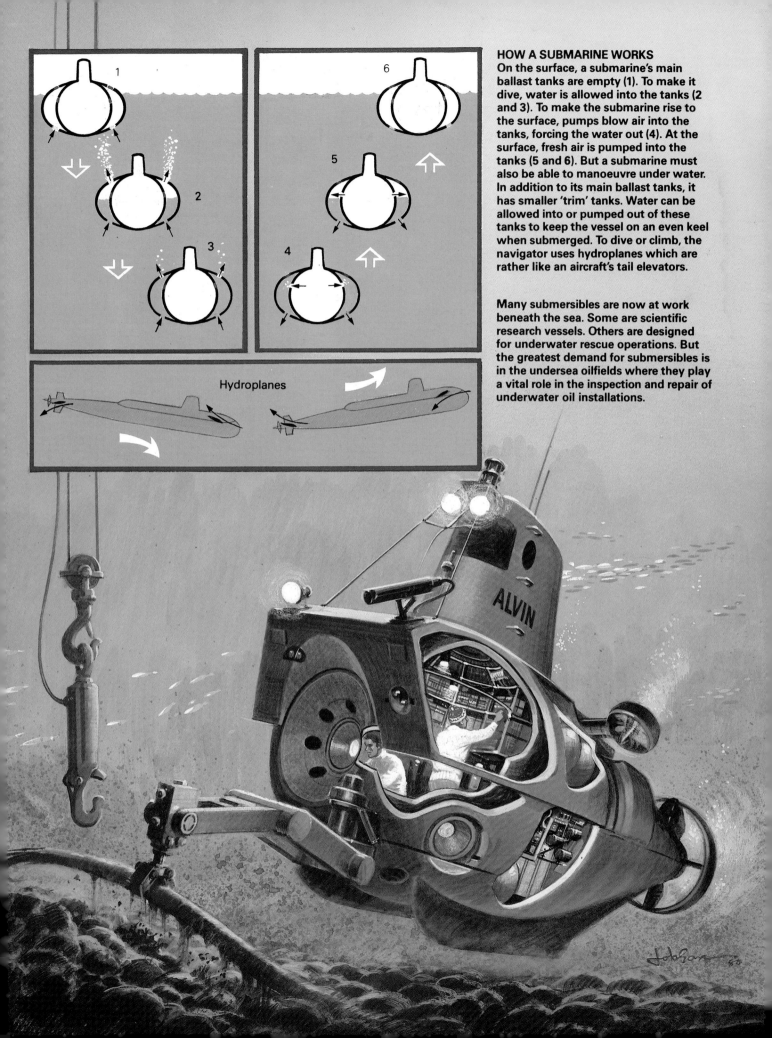

HOW A SUBMARINE WORKS

On the surface, a submarine's main ballast tanks are empty (1). To make it dive, water is allowed into the tanks (2 and 3). To make the submarine rise to the surface, pumps blow air into the tanks, forcing the water out (4). At the surface, fresh air is pumped into the tanks (5 and 6). But a submarine must also be able to manoeuvre under water. In addition to its main ballast tanks, it has smaller 'trim' tanks. Water can be allowed into or pumped out of these tanks to keep the vessel on an even keel when submerged. To dive or climb, the navigator uses hydroplanes which are rather like an aircraft's tail elevators.

Many submersibles are now at work beneath the sea. Some are scientific research vessels. Others are designed for underwater rescue operations. But the greatest demand for submersibles is in the undersea oilfields where they play a vital role in the inspection and repair of underwater oil installations.

Hydroplanes

ALVIN

Heat Engines

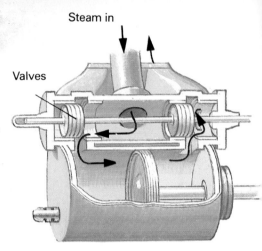

An engine is any machine that takes energy from heat, water or wind and makes this energy do useful work. The windmill and the waterwheel are simple kinds of engine, and people are still trying to make these engines more efficient. Steam engines took the place of the windmill and the waterwheel, and today we have petrol engines, diesel engines, jet engines and turbines.

A steam engine is a *heat engine*. Heat from burning coal, oil or gas is used to turn water in a boiler into steam. When water boils to become steam it expands to about 1,700 times its size. Steam engines use the energy of expanding steam to drive wheels or do other work.

In a simple steam engine a piston slides to and fro inside a hollow cylinder. A system of valves allows steam into the cylinder at one end, then at the other, driving the piston back and forth.

How a Steam Engine Works

In a steam engine, the expanding steam pushes a piston to and fro inside a tube called a cylinder. The piston is attached to a piston rod that moves in and out with the piston. The piston rod is attached to another, longer rod called the connecting rod, which is joined to a driving wheel and makes it go round.

Various systems of valves allow the steam to shoot into the cylinder so that it drives the piston first one way, then the other. This kind of engine is called a *reciprocating* engine. At the beginning of the 1900s the reciprocating engine was the chief source of power. It ran locomotives, ships, factory machines and even motor cars. Today it has almost vanished because more efficient kinds of engines have been invented.

Another kind of steam engine is the *steam turbine*. A turbine is a large wheel with dozens of blades round it. A powerful jet of steam is made to hit the blades and cause the turbine to spin. Spinning turbines can be used to make electricity or drive a ship's propellers.

Internal Combustion

The motor car engine is called an *internal combustion* engine because the fuel is burned inside the engine. (In the steam engine the fuel is burned outside, away from the moving parts.) The internal combustion engine is more efficient than the steam engine. It gives more power for the energy put into it.

How it Works

The fuel – petrol or diesel oil – burns in a hollow cylinder. As the fuel turns to gas, it expands and

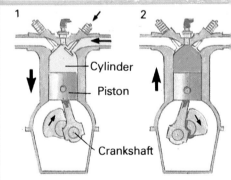

Petrol engines do not give power on every stroke of the piston. The diagrams above show what happens. At (1) an inlet valve opens and a mixture of petrol and air is sucked into the cylinder. Then the valve closes and as the piston goes

pushes a tight-fitting piston down the cylinder. When the piston is pushed down, it turns a *crankshaft*. The crankshaft is made to turn the car's wheels.

The Wankel Engine

The Wankel engine is an internal combustion engine like the ordinary petrol engine, but there are no pistons moving in cylinders. Instead of pistons, the Wankel has a central rotor in the shape of a triangle with curved sides. As the rotor goes round the combustion chamber, the engine goes through the intake, compression, power and exhaust stages of an ordinary engine.

Jet Engines

There are several kinds of jet engine. The first to be invented, and still very much used, is the *turbojet*, pictured in the diagram below. It works by eating up air in enormous quantities – it needs the oxygen in the air to make the fuel burn properly. As air is sucked in at the front by a series of fast-spinning blades, it is *compressed* – squeezed into a small space. The air has to be compressed to give a lot of oxygen in the combustion chamber.

Special paraffin is sprayed into the combustion chamber. This fuel spray goes on all the time the engine is working. It is first ignited

The engine above is a *turboprop*. In this engine the turbojet is used to turn a propeller which drives the aircraft forward. The turboprop is used on smaller aircraft, in which it is most efficient.

The *turbofan* engine pictured below is the one that powers most of today's big airliners. These engines have huge fans at the front to push enormous quantities of air back into the compressor. The air is divided into two streams; one goes through the combustion chamber, the other flows past the engine itself. The two streams combine at the back to give greater thrust.

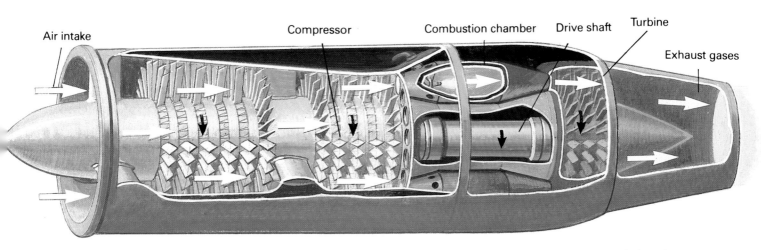

Air intake — Compressor — Combustion chamber — Drive shaft — Turbine — Exhaust gases

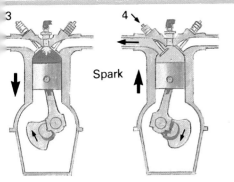

up it squeezes the fuel into the top of the cylinder (2). A spark takes place and the fuel mixture burns with great force and pushes the piston down the cylinder (3). Then an exhaust valve opens and the burnt gases are pushed out (4).

by electric sparks. As the fuel burns, its temperature rises to well over 1000°C. The hot gases expand and shoot out backwards into the atmosphere. This powerful stream of hot gas shooting out pushes the aircraft forward.

The hot gases turn another wheel called a *turbine*. A shaft connects the turbine to the compressor. This means that the compressor is kept turning and squeezing more air into the engine.

Jet speeds are sometimes increased by burning extra fuel between the turbine and the outlet nozzle. This is called *afterburning*.

The Wankel engine

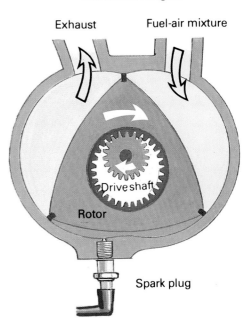

Exhaust — Fuel-air mixture — Drive shaft — Rotor — Spark plug

Radio and Television

Inside the Camera

The job of a television camera is to turn the image it sees into electrical signals that can be transmitted. In colour TV, the camera usually has three separate tubes inside it. These tubes split up the light from the image into three parts – a red part, a green part and a blue part. This splitting up is done by special mirrors called *dichroic mirrors*. You can see how this works in the diagram on the opposite page.

Each light colour goes through a special tube in the camera. These tubes make a pattern of electric charge as light falls on them. A beam of electrons in each tube moves quickly over the pattern of electric charge, going from left to right and top to bottom. This is called scanning. It makes a stream of electric signals, each signal telling how bright or dark a tiny part of the whole picture is.

From the Studio to Your Home

Several cameras are used to give different views of whatever is being televised. The cameras turn the image of what they see into electrical signals. These signals are fed to a control room where the programme director sits in front of a row of TV screens. Each screen shows the picture from one of the

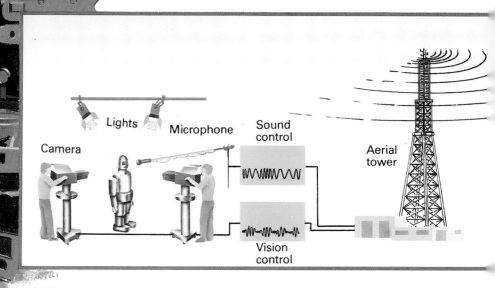

Lights Microphone Sound control

Camera

Vision control

Aerial tower

Radio Waves

Radio waves are quite invisible, but we know that they can be of many different wavelengths. (The wavelength is the distance between the top of one hump in the wave and the top of the next hump.) Some are very short – only a few centimetres long, others can be several kilometres long. Unlike sound waves, radio waves do not need air to travel through. We can talk to astronauts on the Moon because the radio waves travel quite easily through empty space. When a radio wave hits the aerial of your radio, it sets up a tiny electric current. If the set is tuned to the wavelength of the radio wave, the circuits in the set get rid of the carrier wave and send the signals of a person's voice or music to your loudspeaker.

cameras. The director chooses which picture he wants at a particular time, and the signals from this picture are fed to the transmitter. The transmitter may be quite a long way away from the studio.

Sound in the studio is picked up by microphones – again there can be several. The microphones turn the sound into electrical signals which go to a sound mixing position in the control room. There the sounds are selected or mixed as required before being fed to the transmitter.

The vision and sound signals are carried on radio waves sent out from the aerial at the top of the big tower. These radio waves are picked up by a receiving aerial and go into your TV set. The set turns the signals back into pictures and sound that you can see and hear.

Inside Your TV Set

When the picture signals go into your TV set they are removed from the radio wave that has carried them, and go into a cathode ray tube. You look at the front of this tube when you watch TV. An electron gun for each colour shoots out electrons which strike the back of the screen. This is covered with different types of tiny phosphor dots that glow blue, red or green when they are hit. The dots form the image you see.

Satellite TV

Orbiting satellites transmit television pictures world-wide.

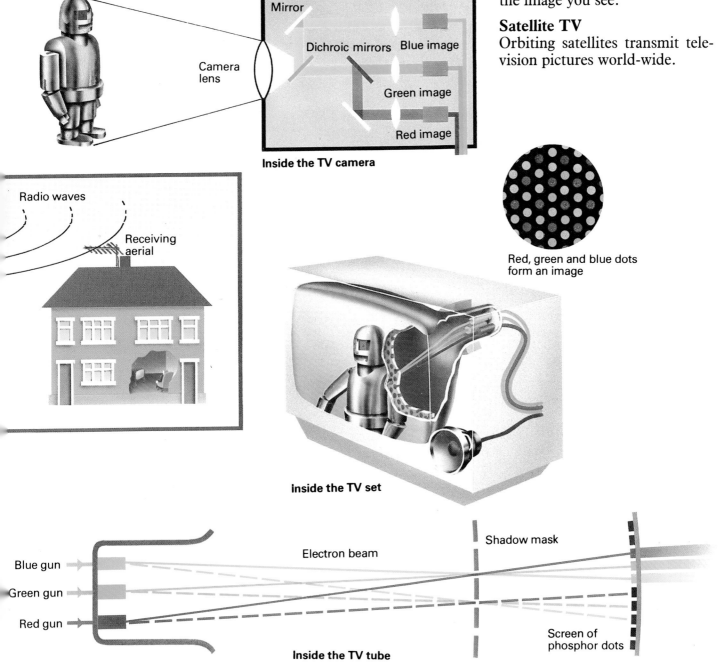

Inside the TV camera

Mirror

Dichroic mirrors Blue image

Camera lens

Green image

Red image

Radio waves

Receiving aerial

Red, green and blue dots form an image

inside the TV set

Blue gun

Green gun

Red gun

Electron beam

Shadow mask

Screen of phosphor dots

Inside the TV tube

39

Computers and Robots

Computers are playing a more and more important part in all our lives, whether we realize it or not. Businesses, large and small, are using computers to keep accounts, pay salaries, keep an eye on the stock position. They are used in schools, by the police, by banks, by the armed forces, by airlines and by scientists.

The strange thing is that computers can only do a few simple tasks. They can add. They can subtract. And they can compare one number with another. Why, then, are computers so special. The answer is that they can do these three things at lightning fast speed. They can do millions of calculations in a second.

Although the computer works with numbers, the information it uses does not have to start off as numbers. It can play chess with you, guide a spacecraft, check fingerprints and draw a map of Australia. But before it begins to work on any of these tasks it turns the information into numbers. And the numbers it uses are not quite the same as ours. We use the numbers 0 to 9. All the computer needs is 0 and 1. In fact, it can only count up to 1! This is called the *binary system*.

The computer uses the binary system because it has been designed to work with electrical currents. It can recognize the difference between a flow of current and no flow of current. If there is a current it registers 1; if there is no current it registers 0.

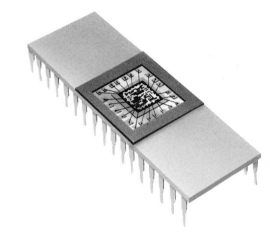

At the heart of every computer, pocket calculator or digital watch is the silicon chip. A tiny chip only 5 mm square, can be the main part of a computer. The number of microscopic transistors and other electrical parts that can be put on a chip has increased rapidly year by year. It is now possible to put more than a million of them on a single tiny chip.

Because the silicon chip is so small and cheap, computers have also become much smaller and cheaper.

As we press the computer's keys to give it commands, the computer translates our key commands into its own binary computer language and works on them. The result appears on the screen.

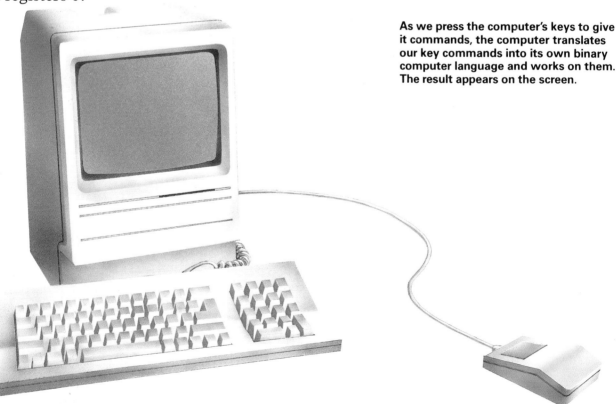

Communicating with the Computer

To instruct a computer to do something you have to write a program. Writing a program in binary numbers would take a lot of time and effort – the binary for our 8 is 1000 and to the computer the letter T is 01010100. So a simple solution has been found. The computer itself is programmed to translate our instructions into binary. We type in our program in a language we can understand. The computer then translates our language into its own language and starts work on it.

The computer does all its calculations in its main part – called the *central processing unit* or CPU for short. It also has a memory where it stores all the information that is fed into it. It stores little bits of information in separate memory locations or 'boxes'. All we have to do is give the computer the address of any memory location and the machine will find the information in that location in a millionth of a second.

To communicate with a computer we usually type in letters and numbers as on an ordinary typewriter, but using some special computer commands.

WHAT IS A ROBOT?

A robot is a machine that can be programmed to do different tasks. And most robots have an arm or arms that can do work for us. The robot's master is a computer.

More and more robots are working in factories all over the world. They spray paint, lift heavy loads and weld things together. And when they have been taught to do these things they usually do them better than human beings can. Switch on a robot and it will go on working 24 hours a day without stopping for a rest. It can work in places where people could not exist, and it hardly ever goes sick.

In the picture below, robots are welding cars as they move along an assembly line. Very careful programming lies behind a production system like this. A computer controls the robots so that they spot weld sections of each car without getting in each other's way.

Journeys into Space

On March 16, 1926, an American scientist, Dr Robert Goddard, fired the first liquid-fuelled rocket into space. Goddard's rocket rose only 60 metres into the air, but this was the first tiny step towards bigger and more powerful rockets that took people to the Moon and probes right out of our Solar System.

A mere 31 years after Goddard's rocket, the Russians launched Sputnik 1, the first man-made satellite to orbit the Earth. This happened on October 4, 1957, and it was on that day that the Space Age began. Since then, hundreds of satellites have been fired into space and the Shuttle blasts off into space and lands back on Earth with an ease we are now beginning to take for granted.

Probes to the Planets

Some of the most exciting space projects have been the unmanned probes sent up to find out more about other planets in our Solar System. In 1976, two *Viking* spacecraft landed on Mars. They carried out tests to find out whether any form of life existed on the Red Planet; but they could find none.

Vostok 1 **was the Russian one-man spacecraft in which Yuri Gagarin made the first ever manned flight into space (1). He blasted off on 12 April 1961.**

The Americans who landed on the Moon travelled in *Apollo* **craft (2). The Command Module for the men was in the nose of the spacecraft.**

Venera 4 **(3) was one of several Russian craft that reached Venus and released a capsule by parachute (right). The** *Veneras* **radioed back to Earth several important discoveries.**

American *Pioneer* **probes (4) flew close to Jupiter in 1973 and 1974. They took some remarkable close-up pictures of the giant planet.**

A *Viking* **Mars craft is seen at (5).**

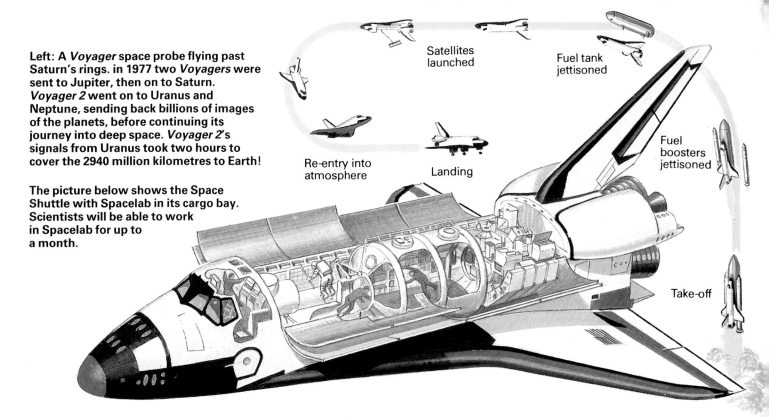

Left: A *Voyager* space probe flying past Saturn's rings. in 1977 two *Voyagers* were sent to Jupiter, then on to Saturn. *Voyager 2* went on to Uranus and Neptune, sending back billions of images of the planets, before continuing its journey into deep space. *Voyager 2*'s signals from Uranus took two hours to cover the 2940 million kilometres to Earth!

The picture below shows the Space Shuttle with Spacelab in its cargo bay. Scientists will be able to work in Spacelab for up to a month.

Satellites launched

Fuel tank jettisoned

Fuel boosters jettisoned

Re-entry into atmosphere

Landing

Take-off

The Space Shuttle

When the Space Shuttle *Columbia* blasted off in 1981 a new kind of space travel began. After a flight of 54½ hours in space, it glided back to a perfect landing on a desert airstrip.

Before the Shuttle, all rockets and manned spacecraft were used only once. This made space flight very expensive. The Space Shuttle is a combined launch rocket and spacecraft that can be used many times.

The Shuttle is launched by rocket like other spacecraft, but it glides back to land on a runway like an aircraft. It has three main rocket engines which are fed with fuel from a big tank. This tank is dumped when all its fuel is gone. Two extra rockets are attached to the sides of the Shuttle to help it into space. These rockets fall away as the ship climbs, and drop by parachute into the ocean. There they are recovered and can be used again. As the Shuttle glides back through the atmosphere, special tiles protect it from the fierce heat.

Tomorrow's World

The world we live in is changing faster than ever before. The invention of robots and the microchip is bringing about a revolution in the industrial countries. In years to come people should have a better standard of living, better health, better education, and far more leisure time.

But there are many problems facing mankind in the future. There are many millions of people in the poorer countries who do not have enough to eat. Many cannot read or write and they have little medical care. It will take many years and much effort to make their lives anything like as comfortable as our own.

Below: As the Earth's supplies of metals run out it is possible that other planets and their moons will be mined. The metals will be refined in space and then brought back to Earth.

Bottom: There are many schemes to harness the energy of the waves. One scheme involves large tanks or 'ducks' being rocked up and down by the waves. The motion of the tanks would be used to drive an electricity generator.

In richer countries there are other problems. The consumption of energy and raw materials, for instance, is so great that the Earth is running short of many of its riches. Unless vast new oilfields are found the world will run out of gasoline within thirty years at the present rate of consumption. And the supply of certain metals such as copper and tin will last little longer. That is why scientists are searching for alternative sources of energy, such as harnessing the heat of the Sun and the motion of the waves. For the same reason the recycling of materials will become more important.

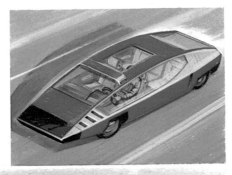

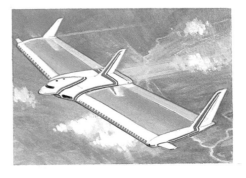

Above: The shape of tomorrow's transport is already on the drawing boards. The main feature of all the designs is that they will use as little energy as possible.

Below: In the future self-supporting colonies will probably be established in space. They may take the form of huge spinning rings. The spin would create artificial gravity for the colonists.

Index

Illustrators
Mike Atkinson, Jim Dugdale, Ron Jobson, Janos Marffy,
John Marshall, Bernard Robinson, Frederick St. Ward,
Mike Saunders and David Wright.

Cover illustrations by
Brian Watson/Linden Artists

British Library Cataloguing in Publication Data

Dempsey, Michael W. (Michael William)
    The World of science.
    I. Title
    500

    ISBN 0-7235-4320-8

Copyright © 1990 World International Publishing Limited.
All rights reserved. Published in Great Britain by
World International Publishing Limited,
an Egmont Company, Egmont House, PO Box 111,
Great Ducie Street, Manchester M60 3BL.

Printed in Singapore.

ISBN 0 7235 4320 8